The Politics of the Texas Sheriff:

From Frontier to Bureaucracy

James G. Dickson

AMERICAN PRESS
Boston, Massachusetts

Cover Photo: Past Presidents of Sheriffs Association of Texas, 101st Annual Conference, 1979.
Courtesy: *The Texas Lawman.*

Copyright © 1983 by American Press.

All rights reserved. No part of this publication may be reproduced, stored in a retrieval system, or transmitted, in any form or by any means, electronic, mechanical, photocopying, recording, or otherwise, without the prior written permission of the copyright owner.

Printed in the United States of America.

Preface

The TEXAS HISTORY SERIES of American Press consists of original essays about Texas history written primarily for undergraduates. The series examines a wide variety of topics, some traditional such as Hispanic colonization, the Texas Revolution, or Reconstruction; others address topics that are usually minimized or ignored such as women in Texas, organized labor, or cultural diversity.

The series will be topically complete for courses in Texas History. It has no limits. Instead, it will be continually added to in response to new research and as gaps in our list are identified. This approach will keep the list current and fresh, and its freshness will be enhanced by our technology which permits authors to make changes in their published essays as needed.

Each essay may be purchased separately, allowing professors to choose those essays appropriate to their specific courses and emphases. The cost of each book has been kept very low. This series makes it possible to select a topically complete and well organized set of books at a total cost very competitive with the inflexible textbooks currently available. Several essays may even be bound into one volume and provide additional savings for your students without compromising the quality of your course.

The TEXAS HISTORY SERIES is designed to offer the freshest possible course materials in a format that permits flexibility for instructors and economy for students. We believe it offers a unique alternative to standard texts.

ROBERT J. ROSENBAUM
Editor

Contents

Historical Background of the Office 1
    English Roots 1
    The Sheriff Comes to America 5
    The Sheriff Moves West 7

Institutional Dynamics of the Texas Sheriff 9
    Selection and Perquisites 9
    Power and Duties 11
    Organizational Patterns and Administration 17

A Demographic Profile of the Texas Sheriff 19
    Connecting the Dots of the Composite Portrait   28

The Political Dynamics of the Texas Sheriff 29
    The Sheriff as Political Microcosm 33
    Rural Sheriffs: Findings and Impressions 36
    Urban Sheriffs - Perceptions 42
    The Politics of Intergovernmental Relations 45
    General Conclusions on the Politics
      of the Sheriff 49

**The Human Dimension of the Office:
From Two-Fisted, Two-Gun Days to Modern
Technological Professional** 50
    Dramatis Personae 54

Concluding Observations 63

Suggested Additional Readings 65
    British Background 65
    General Works on the American Sheriff and the
      Sheriff of Other States 65
    The Texas Sheriff 67

Historical Background of the Office

The image of the American sheriff fluctuates between extremes. Public perceptions alternate between Hollywood concoctions of the quiet, courageous, bigger-than-life heroes portrayed by Gary Cooper and Henry Fonda, and blustery, profane, and ineffectual fools such as Buford T. Justice, as roared by Jackie Gleason, supposedly the sheriff of Texarkana, in the film *Smoky and the Bandit*. Anyone who had ever met the incumbent sheriff of Bowie County at the time of the release of *Smoky and the Bandit* would know how off the mark Gleason's characterization was from the soft-spoken family man then in office. This discrepancy is typical of the history of the American sheriff.

The sheriff has been one of the most important and powerful offices of local government throughout Texas history, but the literature available on the office's real attributes and its roles in our political system is quite sparse. Libraries usually contain stilted biographies of individual sheriffs which tell very little of the institutional and historical characteristics of the office itself.

English Roots

Like most American common law offices, the sheriff is of ancient lineage. Discernible roots of the county sheriff extend back into our British background for more than a thousand years. The shrievalty is, in fact, the oldest office deriving from the appointments of the British monarchy and came about through the efforts of Saxon Kings to create an effective central administration for the British Isles. From its inception, the office was pulled between kings, intent upon centralizing administration in their hands, and the drive on the part of the political subdivisions of Great Britain for more effective home rule.

The structure of British local governments was originally para-military. Seventh Century Anglo-Saxons organized themselves into groups of tens and then into groups of hundreds—at first for war, and then for peacetime administration. Ten families residing together in a *tun* (town) comprised a *tithing*. Each *tithing* selected a leader (tithingman). Ten *tithings* made up a *hundred*. Hundreds came to be headed by a *gerefa*, or chief. Subsequently, the *gerefa* evolved in the Saxon language into a *reeve*. The *gerefa* and the *reeve* became elected officials with both police powers and judicial powers. Under King Alfred the Great (871-901 A.D.), the existing hundreds were formulated into a *scir* (shire). Over each of the *scirs* was placed a headman known as a *reeve*, and later as a *shire-reeve* to make certain that this official was clearly superior to the previous *reeve* of the *hundred*. The *scyre-reeve* (shire-reeve) was the principal administrative representative of the King in each shire as keeper or chief of each shire. The shire was the organizational forerunner of the present-day county.

Under Saxon kings, the sheriff (shire-reeve) became the principal law enforcement officer of the shire, functioning as much as a judge as a policeman. Primarily noblemen, the sheriffs became the king's major peacekeeping and tax collecting agents. In times of military emergency sheriffs also fulfilled military leadership tasks for the king. By the time of the Norman invasion in 1066, the sheriffs had become very important and busy law enforcement, judicial, military, and fiscal instruments of the king's peace.

After 1066, King William centralized administrative institutions and severely modified the locally oriented character of Saxon rule. Altering the elective status of sheriffs, Norman kings utilized them increasingly for gathering tax revenues in their respective shires. In compiling all taxable property in his *Domesday Book* in 1085, King William mentions the office of sheriff at least five times. Norman kings developed the practice of "selling" the shrievalties to nobles willing to pay for the privilege of serving as sheriff, which permitted many opportunities for the incumbent to feather his own financial nest.

King Henry I codified major crimes into a penal code, which further centralized criminal justice in the hands of the king. Sheriffs continued as the major agents of this penal system, enhancing their positions as law enforcement officers. Throughout the succession of royal Houses that followed the last of the Norman kings in the Twelfth Century, the sheriff's scope of authority and variety of royal tasks expanded. The opportunities for abuses of power also magnified. As the House of Plantagenet succumbed to the House of Lancaster, and Lancaster to the House of York, and thence to the House of Tudor and Stuart, the sheriff's roles and power position steadily modified. The authority of the sheriff became more sharply separated from those of other local officials as successive kings tightened their own personal rule. The sheriff's power diminished, particularly in the Fourteenth Century, but the institution itself survived tenaciously.

By the Fourteenth Century, the sheriff's duties were complex, difficult, and increasingly expensive to the incumbent sheriff. In addition to his multifarious duties, the sheriff was responsible for the safe passage of the king through his shire and for feeding and entertaining the sovereign on his progress through his bailiwick. This latter duty was onerous and costly, and when coupled with the requirement that he defray expenses for the conduct of courts held regularly in his jurisdiction, from his own pocket, the drain on personal finances was enormous. Plantagenet kings required the sheriffs to make an accounting of their tax collections, making it more difficult to skim off the top, a frequent abuse of the shrievalty. To be dubbed by the king as the sheriff was an honor local noblemen did not relish. It was folly to refuse and expensive to accept.

By the Eighteenth Century, sheriffs were paid a salary as Keeper of the King's Peace, though this did not make it any easier to enforce the law. Rudimentary police forces and primitive custodial facilities made law enforcement a difficult facet of the sheriff's overall duties. From the Norman kings through the Stuarts, sheriffs were increasingly looked upon by kings as fiscal agents, assuring the collection of the king's revenues. Kings used the sheriffs in combatting the decentralizing forces of the feudal system. Beginning in the Thirteenth Century and continuing into the Fourteenth Century, the sheriffs began a gradual decline in overt power, as the British Parliamentary system began to manifest itself through the spread of the franchise and the proliferation of judicial officials who implemented the great common law system.

By the time the American colonies began to develop their own structures, the British shrievalty was still functional. In the Seventeenth Century, the English sheriff remained the chief executive of the king's local judiciary, the official medium of communication between the central government and the county, and the conservator of the king's peace. Administrative and judicial functions had shrunk, and the once great financial powers were considerably diminished. In fiscal and judicial powers, other local officials had absorbed functions previously the exclusive province of the sheriff. Thus, the English sheriff continued as a figure of local repute and respect, and the office remained one of the principal connecting points between the local and central levels of British government, though its powers were increasingly circumscribed.

The Sheriff Comes to America

The American sheriff first appeared in a form that any Englishman would recognize in 1634 in the Virginia Colony. With minor modifications, the office flourished at approximately the same time in the proprietary colony of Maryland. The colonists were quite familiar with English local government, and as governors and proprietors extended greater home-rule to the newly created shires (counties), local residents transplanted those features of English local government that appeared to be practicable in the new milieu. An important part of this new fabric of local governance was the English sheriff. The colonial sheriff came from the same social strata as in England, that is, from the large landowners. Frequently, these worthies would alternate between appointments as justices of the peace and as sheriff. As in England, the shrievalty could be a lucrative post. From the first, the appointments were made by the colonial governor (or Lord Proprietor), with county commissioners often being influential in the selections. The colonists wanted their sheriffs to possess all the legal rights and powers of his English counterpart, but situational differences produced adaptations almost immediately. The colonial sheriff was recognizable but different, and modifications continue to the present.

Much of the ceremonial pomp of the English sheriff was dropped in the Virginia and Maryland sheriffs. The sheriff's duties as a tax collector and related financial concerns were enhanced in the colonies at a time when these functions were attenuated in the English sheriff. The colonial sheriff collected taxes not only for the king but the numerous poll taxes levied by Parliament. In this area, the sheriff in the colonies was both a royal/proprietary official and a colonial agent, a composite character which would continue to be characteristic of the southern sheriff. Despite this, the colonial sheriff was not subject to the rigid accountability in fiscal matters as the English sheriff, and

American sheriff's, like American counties, functioned more independently of the central government than in England.

As a law enforcer and conservator of the peace, the colonial sheriff made equal use of the *posse comitatus* as his English forebear. In emergency law enforcement situations, the colonial sheriff could enlist the aid of all able-bodied persons in the county, including the use of their weapons, their boats, and their horses. The Virginia sheriff was expected to enforce religious and political conformity among its citizens, as was the English sheriff.

In the colonies where the first efforts were made to establish a local official like the English sheriff, the similarities between the English sheriff and his American model were more numerous than the differences. Among the similarities were: (1) making public proclamations (official medium of communication and official link with central government); (2) supervising and returning elections; (3) executing the administrative and judicial business of the courts; (4) keeping the peace; and (5) assessing and collecting royal and proprietary revenues. With the exception of the excisions of English laws which were irrelevant to the colonial situation, the sheriff performed all his duties in strict conformity to English custom and law. Immediately discarded were certain judicial functions (the courts themselves in which these functions occurred were never transported) and almost the whole bag of ceremonial duties and services. Some of the American sheriff's functions which contributed the most to his power and prestige were declining in the Mother Country, particularly his financial powers. In England the sheriff collected only royal taxes, while parliamentary poll taxes were collected by other agencies. In America, the sheriff was the principal collector for both types of taxes.

As the American sheriff moved westward and southward his divergencies from the English parent institution continued to unfold. The new environment reshaped the institution, leaving out the institutional deadwood of the English sheriff. Some of the early sources of strength in the sheriff, which had declined considerbly in England, would be revitalized. One noteworthy transformation was a gradual democratization of the office.

The major departures between the colonial sheriff and the English sheriff included: (1) increasing the colonial sheriff's financial powers; (2) shrinking the colonial sheriff's judicial powers; (3) a change in election duties (temporary reduction); (4) the colonial sheriff was more purely a local official than a royal, provincial character; (5) the colonial sheriff was more of a democratic office; and (6) the colonial sheriff enjoyed a more important position in county government. The colonial sheriff did not have to exercise many of the social and prestigious ceremonial functions, but his augmented powers in political and economic matters made up for the loss. The colonial sheriff actually regained some of the prestige of his European counterpart as a conservator of the peace. Typically of the entire history of the American sheriff, he would reflect intimately the formative influences that were being generally exerted upon state and county governments.

The Sheriff Moves West

As Americans moved across the Mississippi River, they carried with them the long history of Anglo-American law enforcement practices. The senior member of this heritage was the sheriff, who had already undergone a considerable environmental sculpting by the Tidewater ecology into which it had first been transplanted. The westward spread of the frontier added certain elements to the continuing evolution of American law enforcement agencies, absorbing the effects of the peculiar geographic, cultural, and economic milieu of the West.

Distinctive patterns of lawlessness produced by the spatial and economic circumstances of the West altered the crime fighting situation without substantively changing the devices used by the western settlers to establish order in their new lives. The great cattle and sheep industries became a unique new fountainhead of crime and produced certain distinctive effects on the ancient shrievalty, without really altering its basic nature. Since the states in the South had stressed the importance of the county sheriff, many of the new territories and states in the West, populated by southerners, would emulate the practice. For a time, many of the frontier communities applied practices similar to the medieval English "mutual pledge" and "hue and cry" systems as a means of social code enforcement, before they could establish the ordinary means utilized in the East. From the beginning, the peace officer in the West combined traits of skill and appearance of authority with the political abilities required to get into and remain in office, usually as elected officials.

Texas was one of the first sites where Spanish law enforcement practices met Anglo-American forms. Early Anglo-American colonists used the Spanish-Mexican *comisario* of police. In 1831, San Felipe de Austin established a community patrol (sometimes dubbed the first operating local police agency in the English-speaking West). In Stephen F. Austin's East Texas settlements, an appointed sheriff was utilized as a part of an enforcement system that combined English and Spanish features. The combination of the English sheriff with the Spanish *alguacil* (the Spanish equivalent to the modern sheriff) did not materially alter the powers or the institutional traits of the English model. In the earliest Spanish communities, the *alguacil* was appointed by either the provincial governor or the *ayuntamiento* (local council). The duties of the *alguacil* were recognizable beside modern police functions: patrol duties (especially at night), powers of arrest and custody, and execution of judicial and executive writs were among the stable functions of this local police official. The *alguacil* was assisted by *tenientes,* that is assistants or deputies, within administrative limits not unlike the ancient English-American arrangement.

By the time of Texas' fight for independence from Mexico, the county sheriff was a local figure of considerable power and importance, both politically and professionally. Like his brothers along the eastern seaboard, the developmental rigors of the western frontier revitalized ancient prerogatives within a political environment like the Old South. In every constitution of the nation, territory, and state of Texas, an organic provision was made for the sheriff as a focal point of local law enforcement and administration.

Institutional Dynamics of the Texas Sheriff

Selection and Perquisites

The sheriff was specified by the Texas constitution for each of Texas' 254 counties. A major vestige of Jacksonian democracy in the Texas political system is the election of many public officials, including the sheriff. The voters of each county elect a sheriff for a four-year term from among persons nominated in the two major political parties' primary elections. The constitution is silent with respect to qualifications for candidates for sheriff. Consequently, persons with little or no training have always been able to qualify for the office. Until the past few years, farmers and certain types of small businessmen have tended to dominate the office. Recent years have seen a larger incidence of election of people with greater experience and training as peace officers.

Courtesy of *Bicentennial History of Nacogdoches*

Sheriff A. J. Spradley, Nacogdoches County, 1882-1894, 1896-1898, 1900-1904, 1908-1910, 1914-1916. An example of an "Old West" type of sheriff.

The Constitution authorizes the Texas Legislature to determine the fees, salaries, and perquisites paid to the sheriff and his deputies. For many years, sheriffs were paid primarily through fees paid to the sheriff for each of the principal law enforcement and judicial duties performed by the sheriff or his deputies. The legislature established an *ex officio* salary (very minimal) to be paid to the sheriff, while relying primarily on remuneration by fees. The opportunity for graft and administrative manipulations skirting the outer limits of graft was very great. The lack of uniformity in the financing of sheriffs' activities was enormous during much of the history since 1876.

Since 1973, counties in excess of 20,000 population must compensate sheriffs by salary. Counties with less than 20,000 must decide through their county commissioners whether to pay the sheriff a salary, except that in the small counties where the sheriff still serves as tax assessor and collector, the county must pay the sheriff a salary for this role. The statutes continue a schedule of fees for the sheriff in some of his judicial tasks as officers of the county and district courts.

Vacancies in the office of sheriff between elections are filled by the county commissioners court, which is the principal administrative body of county government.

Power and Duties

The constitutional bases of the sheriff's powers and roles are relatively few and simple. The Constitution creates the office and provides for its continued incumbency within the electoral system of the state. The state legislature shall prescribe the fundamental duties and powers of the sheriff. The Constitution also provides for the removal of the sheriff by the judges of state district courts for incompetency, official misconduct, habitual drunkenness, or other causes defined by law. A jury must

Courtesy of Dallas County Sheriff's Department

Norval R. Winniford
1st "Appointed" Republican Sheriff
Dallas County, 1867

attest to the substantiality of the charges against the sheriff. In counties of very small population, the Constitution provides that the assessment and collection of county and state taxes shall be performed by the sheriff. This latter function is almost of antiquarian interest only since so few counties do not have a separate tax assessor and collector. The fees and compensation of county officers, including the sheriff, are mentioned in the Constitution, although the legislature has the principal responsibility for detailed policy. Interestingly, the sheriff is actually created in the judicial article of the Constitution, though he is typically thought of as an executive agent. There is some historical logic to providing for the sheriff in the judicial article, since the ancient English sheriff's duties were largely judicial in character.

As the designated conservator of the peace for each county, the sheriff is the principal law enforcement officer in every county; his jurisdiction extends literally to the entire county. In practice, the day-to-day outreach of the sheriff's law enforcement, peace-keeping tasks occur principally in the unincorporated areas of the county, with his involvement within the limits of incorporated cities determined by circumstances and agreements with municipal officials. Included in the sheriff's law enforcement purview are the prevention of crime, the investigation of crimes, traffic control on the highways and roads of the county, the arrest and custody of lawbreakers, protection of life and property, and the general enforcement of all state laws.

The Constitution designates the sheriff as the person in charge of the county courthouse and of the county jail. The latter responsibility has always been a major function of the sheriff, and in the last ten years, the sheriff's custodial services have loomed large in his administrative and political tasks. The county jail generally incarcerates persons who have been apprehended and are awaiting trial, persons who have been convicted of a state crime and are

Courtesy of Mrs. J.E. Ericson, Nacogdoches, Texas

Left to right: Bill Burrows, Bill Longley (famous outlaw), Capt. Milton Mast, sheriff, Nacogdoches County, 1873-1880

awaiting transference to the Texas Department of Corrections, and persons who have been sentenced to short terms by county courts. The size of the jail population in larger jails and the pressure from federal courts and the Texas Commission on Jail Standards to improve the quality of jail facilities and services have forced Texas sheriffs to devote an inordinately large amount of time and resources to jail management. County commissioners, who approve the sheriff's budget within the entire county spending program, have also been swept into a difficult involvement in jail administration.

One of the most important functions of the sheriff is his duty as the executive officer of county and state courts. This ancient task, with roots running back into distant English history, requires the sheriff to serve all the writs, subpoenas, summonses, and processes of county and district courts, both in civil and criminal matters. A designated deputy of the sheriff usually acts as bailiff for the courts in the daily processing of cases.

It was once observed that the Texas sheriff is a combination law enforcer, bill collector, and mess sergeant (the latter referring to the sheriff's oversight of the jail and the feeding and care of the prisoners). This description was particularly apt when the sheriff's major source of compensation was fees assessed for each of the major actions taken by the office. The sheriff is a unique composite as a government agent. The sheriff acts simultaneously as an agent of the State of Texas and of the county. The political power base of the sheriff is local; the voters of his county determine whether or not he will assume and keep the office. The laws which the sheriff must enforce are laws enacted by legislative and judicial agencies of the State of Texas. In law enforcement, there is no such thing as county law. County commissioners in Texas do not possess any ordinance powers, in contrast to city commissioners in home-rule cities. An interesting effect of the overall law enforcement patterns in Texas is

Courtesy of Mrs. J.E. Ericson, Nacogdoches, Texas

David Rusk, Nacogdoches County,
1st Sheriff, Republic of Texas, 1837-1846

that state laws are, in a sense, locally interpreted. That means that the local situation and the political and personal concerns that develop in each county have a great deal to do with the intensity and efficiency with which state laws are enforced.

Organizational Patterns and Administration

Sheriffs' departments in Texas range from one-man operations to departments with several hundred personnel and all the features of a large municipal police force. Once elected, the sheriff must post a bond as a surety against the faithful execution of his civil and criminal duties. The sheriff many appoint one or more deputies within the range of statutory limits on the number of deputies for counties within certain population ranges. Sheriff's deputies are imbued with all the law enforcement authority of the sheriff, and the sheriff is responsible for their actions. State law requires deputies to fulfill certain training tasks in order to be certified as peace officers. The elected sheriff is exempt from such qualifications. Deputies are paid by their respective counties from the sheriff's budget, approved by the county commissioners.

In 1929, the legislature authorized the creation in counties with populations over 210,000 of a county police force, consisting of at least six patrolmen, appointed by the sheriff, with one designated as the chief of the county police. Implementation of this discrete unit has been negligible, and units of the sheriff's department generally perform patrol and other field services in the county.

Several things affect the organizational patterns of a sheriff's department. Most important are the tax base and population levels of the county, which shape the size of the overall county budget. The only real control which county commissioners have over a sheriff is the power to determine his annual operating funds. Sheriffs are often hard-pressed to convince skeptical and penurious commissioners that they need what they ask for. A mini-confrontation in one smaller county once occurred when the commissioners refused to provide a sheriff additional funds for gasoline for patrol cars. The sheriff ostentatiously cancelled all patrol activities. Groups of citizens passed the hat for the sheriff's gas, and the commissioners finally relented and "found" some more money. In numerous instances, the commissioners remain adamant and do not authorize more money.

Most multi-person sheriff's departments will have a chief deputy, designated by the sheriff. The complexity of a department beyond this specification will depend upon the size of the county, its budget, and related factors. Larger departments will have a hierarchy of ranks similar to the military and to municipal police forces. The chief deputy is second in command and serves as the principal executive officer and administrator, with whatever other duties the sheriff may assign. Descending ranks are usually in charge of sub-divisions of the office; for example: a major may head an operational bureau, a captain may head an operational division, and a lieutenant may supervise a particular watch, assisted by a sergeant. The sheriff tries to assure that every departmental operation has a single, clearly designated person in charge, with lines of authority that clearly run to the sheriff himself.

In addition to the obvious bases for diversity among the sheriffs' departments across the state (population, financial resources, and geographic size), there are other indices of diversity which affect the total character of the office in Texas. For instance, there are strong rural versus urban differences, some of which will be discussed later. There are also regional differences, particularly on an east-west basis. As one progresses further westward in Texas, the character of the sheriff, the tasks which he performs, and the general working environment change. The sheriff is probably more active in the eastern parts of the state. It is difficult to determine why this is so, except that the sparser populations of the western counties may be largely behind this phenomenon.

A Demographic Profile of the Texas Sheriff

A government agency duplicated 254 times, across a huge expanse of territory, with a multiplicy of resources and a constantly changing working environment is not easy to capture in an accurate portrait. The topical subject matter needed to construct a composite image is as varied as the individual and institutional components of the office. A composite of the sheriff in the first years of the 1980s might include personal-biographical items, institutional-departmental items, and law enforcement items. Under personal-biographical could be noted such things as longevity in office, prior law enforcement experience, prior non-law enforcement experience, age, educational background, and prior elective offices held. Institutional-departmental items might include departmental work distribution, department size, civil service requirements for deputies, hours worked by deputies, jail administration, and budget size. Under law enforcement activities, one might list patrol practices and patterns, felony arrest statistics, crime records practices, extent of crime lab facilities, and automotive and communications facilities.

A questionnaire survey of Texas sheriffs administered by the author in the latter years of the 1970s resulted in a return of the survey instrument by a bit over forty-five percent of Texas' 254 sheriffs. A summary view of responses permits an outline of the Texas sheriff as the cumulative transformations of the 1970s thrust the office into the 1980s. The composite portrait is an image of a model, but it permits a tuning in on the profile of an office that has been constantly changing in Texas for more than a hundred years, as it might appear in the latter decades of the Twentieth Century. The disclaimer should be entered that percentages stated are arithmetically rounded, since all respondent sheriffs did not answer every item presented, and all sheriffs did not even return the questionnaire.

The longevity patterns indicated by the respondents showed the following distribution of length of service as sheriff:

> Under five years - 1%
> Between five and ten years - 54%
> Between ten and fifteen years - 10%
> Between fifteen and twenty years - 19%
> Between twenty and twenty-five years - 5%
> Between twenty-five and thirty years - 7%
> Over thirty years - 3%

There appears to be a noteworthy level of experience among the sheriffs of Texas. When considered with other data, the professional caliber of the incumbents is enhanced, in spite of the fact that the law does not require any previous law enforcement experience.

Seventy-nine percent of sheriffs indicated some prior law enforcement experience before their election. Forty-eight percent had been a deputy sheriff, twenty-one percent were former municipal police officers, and eleven percent served with the State Department of Public Safety. Much smaller proportions of sheriffs had been chiefs of police, constables, military police, game wardens, county juvenile officers, guards with the Texas Department of Corrections, investigators for the State Liquor Control Board, district attorneys, deputy United States marshalls, and private security agents. There are fewer grounds for the frequent criticism of the sheriff twenty years ago that too many incumbents had entered the office with no real conception of what would be required of the office. One veteran sheriff observed that when he was first elected to his rural sheriff's post, all he had was a box of keys and no knowledge of what they were supposed to lock and unlock.

When queried about their occupational experience in non-law enforcement fields, the sheriffs indicated a variety of work experience as oil field workers, farmers and ranchers (a healthy 21%), mechanics, factory workers and various types of self-employment and private business. During the 1930s, certain types of small businessmen and farmers tended to dominate the office.

A composite cross-section of the ages of incumbent sheriffs as the 1970s gave way to the 1980s showed the following distribution:

>Under thirty - 1%
>Between thirty and forty - 24%
>Between forty and fifty - 35%
>Between fifty and sixty - 29%
>Between sixty and seventy - 6%
>Over seventy - 3%

These statistics suggest the increasingly noticeable tendency for the office to be held by relatively younger persons.

With regard to the educational background of Texas sheriffs the following patterns were revealed:

>Elementary education only - 4%
>High school diplomas - 32%
>Attended high school, no diploma - 39%
>Some college - 18%
>Bachelor's degree - 6%
>More than 16 years schooling - 3%
>Master's degree - 1 sheriff

Considering what the figures might have shown twenty to thirty years ago, the proportion of sheriffs with considerable educational background is worthy of note.

The level of pre-election education in Texas sheriffs is on the increase. This is significant when coupled with the great likelihood that state law will probably require greater professional law enforcement qualifications for the elected sheriffs within the next few years.

A very small number of the sheriffs had held other elective offices before becoming sheriff, roughly approximating fourteen percent of respondents. A very evenly distributed incidence of service had occurred as: city councilman, school board member, constable, county clerk, tax assessor-collector, justice of the peace, county commissioner, and district clerk.

Sheriffs were asked to record the approximate percentage of the total work time of their departments devoted to law enforcement, traffic duties, court services, jail administration, tax collection, and other duties. There was a significant variety in the responses, with the only consistent factor being the lion's share of work time given to law enforcement, court services, and jail duties; this trio pretty well epitomizes the work of the modern sheriff. Time devoted to law enforcement duties ran the gamut from ninety percent to ten percent; court services ranged from forty-five percent to five percent; jail duties fluctuated from sixty percent to six percent; and traffic functions from fifty-five percent to zero percent.

The spectrum on work distribution naturally reflects department size. Sheriffs were asked to show department size by giving the number of their full-time civilian employees and their full-time sworn deputies. As might be expected, the numbers ran from a one-man department, with one civilian employee to departments of several hundred people. The average sheriff's departments are relatively small, the average being elevated by the huge departments in the metropolitan counties.

With regard to the administration of law enforcement personnel, only eight responding departments said that they provided civil service systems for deputies. Current state law expands the possibility of such a system. Sixty-four departments required newly appointed deputies to serve a probationary period, running from three months to one year. The number of hours per day that deputies were required to work extended from the typical eight-hour day to one respondent requiring a sixteen-hour day. In between these extremes, most of the deputies worked a nine or ten-hour day. Fifty-five percent of sheriff's deputies put in the traditional five-day work week; thirty percent worked a six-day week, thirteen percent worked all seven days each week, while three percent endured a four-day week.

Virtually all sheriff's deputies are covered by federal social security programs. Eighty-five percent of deputies participated in some sort of public retirement system. Seventy-five percent of deputies were covered by accidental death insurance, and sixty-six percent enjoyed insurance coverage for job-connected disabling injuries.

Under the heading "institutional-law enforcement," one observes a wide spectrum of differences among sheriff's departments in such categories as: training programs for deputies (beyond those required by state law for peace officer certification); yearly jail populations; whether or not the sheriff still maintained a residence in the jail; whether his office were in the jail or the courthouse; date of construction of the jail; budget size; number of felony arrests in a year; crime records maintenance; numbers of vehicles maintained; communications systems; special weapons practices; and the like. The responses to these items afford insights into the scope and growing modernity of the sheriff's activities throughout the state, as well as revealing the continuing impact on the institutional face of the office of variances in county size and demographic divergencies.

Seventy-four percent of sheriffs maintained regular, daily road patrols of some sort in their county. Of this group, seventy-two percent sent their daily patrols on

Sheriff J. E. "Bill" Decker, 1951 with Dick West; retired from Dallas Morning News

county rural roads; sixty-one percent covered interstate highways in their counties; forty-six percent included city streets in their bailiwick; and seven percent also included a miscellaneous patrolling of such places as: private roads, rural towns, suburban cities without police forces, oil field roads, and private roads on large ranches.

Every governmental official discovers that how he operates is largely determined by conjunction with other governmental agencies. The skill with which these contacts are handled affects the success of each official. On a year-in-year-out basis, the county commissioners court, presided over by the county judge, is of primary importance in terms of the intergovernmental relations of the Texas sheriff. When asked how often they personally attended meetings of the county commissioners, the sheriffs' responses distributed thusly: thirty-one percent noted that they *always* attended such meetings; thirty-eight percent *usually* attended; fourteen percent attended *infrequently;* fifteen percent attended only *when summoned;* and two percent affirmed that they *never* went to commissioners' sessions.

Sheriffs were asked if they had a definite understanding with municipal police departments in their county with regard to law enforcement responsibilities. Ninety-two percent of sheriffs did have an explicit meeting of the minds with their counterparts in the municipal police establishments concerning the distribution of authority and the law enforcement workload. Within this general affirmation, fifty-four percent of sheriffs stated that they *jointly* enforced the law with the city police within the municipalities of their counties. Thirty-six percent of sheriffs assisted municipal police *only* when called upon to do so or when actually witnessing a law violation. Other arrangements were specified between the sheriff and the Department of Public Safety, a few consolidated law enforcement systems in counties with very few incorporated cities, and extended sheriff's responsibilities in those counties with no municipal police forces.

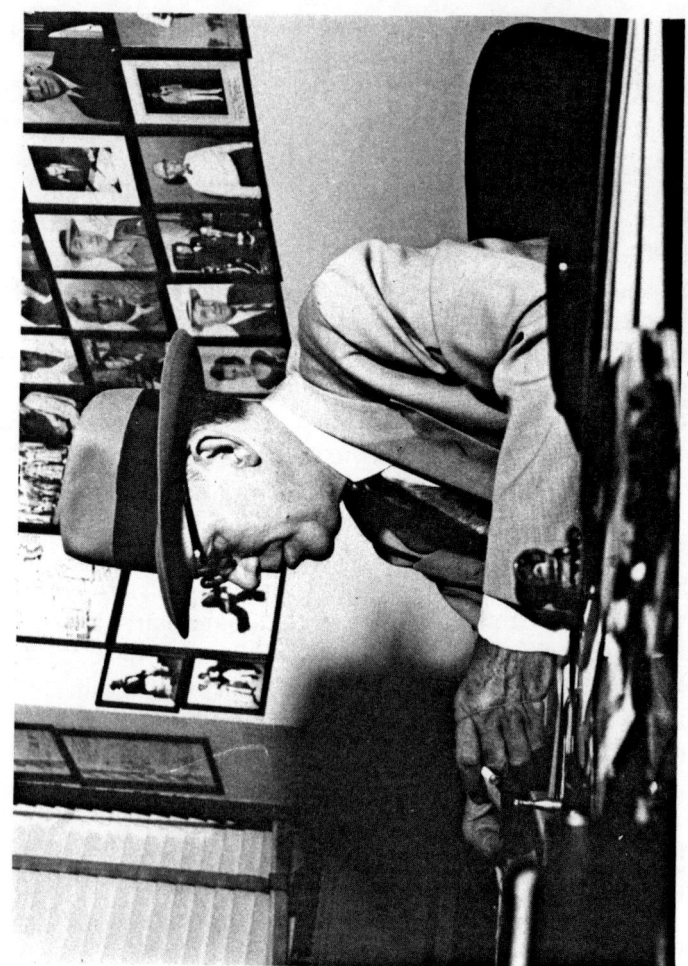

Sheriff Bill Decker, Dallas County, 1949-1970.

The Politics of the Texas Sheriff 27

"Legendary" Bill Decker of Dallas County, 1949-1970

Connecting the Dots of the Composite Portrait

A composite portrait of the Texas sheriff at the transition from the seventies into the eighties might look something like this: a man between thirty and fifty years of age, who had been in office for at least one full term, with considerable law enforcement experience, at least a high school education, and no prior experience in elective office. Under his tutelage would be at least a dozen or more certified peace officers, with a supporting staff of non-uniformed civilians of comparable size. The Constitution of Texas makes him the principal law enforcement officer in his county, although the incorporation of additional territory into municipal jurisdictions every year constricts the area over which his *de facto* responsibilities range.

The work of his department now consumes a much larger share of county budget funds, and the proportion is growing every year; this growth is largely caused by enormous augmentation of his jail responsibilities; plus the twin impact of urban growth and rising crime rates. Recent months have seen the retirement of some of the sheriffs with the longest tenure of office, amounting in some instances to over thirty years. It will be very interesting to see if subsequent elections bring into office a new breed of person to be sheriff—one with more formal education and professional certification training (perhaps required by state law). As the pressure for professionalization grows, there should be a sizable nucleus of professional experience upon which to build.

The Political Dynamics of the Texas Sheriff

Every public official learns that his operational discretion is determined in conjunction with other governmental agencies. For elected public officers, the omnipresent possibility of voter recriminations affects the character of his conduct. The likelihood of contradictory pressures simultaneously pushing the official in different directions goes with the territory in electoral politics. The institutionalization of conflict is endemic to the American political system.

We have blended together a host of conflicting principles in our constitutional crucible. We expect elected officials to live up to them all, even though our constitutions incorporate these contradictions without providing any easy means of reconciling them. Illustrative of this situation are the arcane and scattered provisions of the Texas Constitution pertaining to county government. It is possible to paraphrase Churchill's assertion that the Soviet Union was a "riddle wrapped in a mystery inside an enigma" by characterizing Texas county government as a conflict wrapped in contradiction inside a paradox.

Our separation of powers forces public agencies with independent bases of power and competing goals to share resources from the same larder and resolve problems together from different starting points. No matter how divided their authority and diffuse their financial support, as a matter of efficiency and public accountability there must be someone, somewhere to say: "Do it this way, and now!" Such leadership is difficult under the best of circumstances, where experience and consensus provide solutions based on established compromises. Where a radically new priority is forced upon the system, probably from the outside, the potential for policy conflict, stalemate, and a clouding of the public interest is serious.

We are a very legalistic people. We place confidence in written constitutions and in concrete and elaborate procedural networks operating through complex mechanisms. Rigidly formal specifications of policy for all public processes lend us a great complacency toward the eventual result of governmental actions. We have literally come to believe the old exhortation: "There ought to be a law!" We assume that once there is a law in some area, that is the end of it. Often, it is forgotten that public policy (what governments do and do not do) is not a process of computerized programming with a litmus paper test for the efficacy of what is done. Government enterprises stem from the blending of conflicting individul and group demands in the infinitely changing bargaining of politics.

The fabric of Texas county government provides an excellent specimen of all the semi-myths of politics. One of the comforting aphorisms of American politics is that those governments which are closest to the people (local and state governments) are the most responsible and responsive to public needs. Typically, one finds a sufficient accuracy in this intellectual sedative to foreclose scrutiny of its in-grown fallacies. In Texas county governments, one should ask: "Closest to whom?"

Within the context of daily county government, politics refers to the agreement that is built and rebuilt when all competing groups have made the concessions they are going to make on an issue, producing a watered down form of each participant's wishes. People are often guilty of the naive assumption that a state law establishing some county operation will be enough to achieve fully effective administration. The detailed, restrictive nature of the Texas Constitution on county government perpetuates certain myths about county government and politics.

When trying to understand American governments, it is tempting to look only at the formal aspects, that is, those specifically stated, concretely written provisions that govern policy making. The beginning student of American politics easily makes the mistake of considering only the external, formal attributes of county government, which presents a limited and inaccurate picture of reality. The informal and the political may be more often important in the behavior of officials and institutions; this involves unstated, even unexpected interplays of relationships, demands, and supports that revolve around every major county official. Daily public administration is really a constant adaptation of expectations to reality, the molding of the desirable into the possible, that oils the machinery of county government in Texas...or anywhere else.

In the politics of administration, county officials constantly make adjustments to and revise their perceptions of interest groups which shape routine activities. The process is simply (not easily) answering in the most practical manner the question of "who gets what, where, and how?" In the struggle over scarce resources that embodies the governmental process, this question is constantly raised, and answers are sought. Informal powers involve a discretion that is the mainstay of all public officials, as they try to do what they can with what they have. The instantaneous choosing of alternative ways of getting things done is most graphically noticeable among law enforcement officers in the field. Life-or-death choices are not always prevalent even in law enforcement, but all county officers and deputies face unique choices of action as a part of their daily work. These choices are not always recognized in the formal statement of powers and duties for a governmental position. Without the informal accommodations of formal prescriptions, county government could not function.

Elected officials cannot afford to stray too far from an awareness of the next election, or how daily exercise of discretion might affect reelection chances. In American elections, there are no medals for second place; this is a maxim that is immutable and may be read as an unchallengeable principle. The first ingredient of success for any American statesman, on whatever level of government, is success as an electoral politician. To approach such success, one must walk a tight rope between conflicting demands of persons and groups that comprise the elected official's primary constituency.

Demands exerted on public officials are often based upon the selfish, personal motivations of the constituent, assumed in the constituent's mind to be for "the good of the country." The lobbyist may be grossly ignorant about what the petitioned official really does or really can do. The official must decide if a response is really called for, even if there is not much coincidence between the lobbyist's own welfare and the general good.

Each actor in a drama of county politics is alternately a power or a pawn in the local political game, not always able to act independently in every situation. Some participants are always pawns. The irreducible response for county officials is conducting their tasks efficiently for everyone demanding aid and comfort, without raising taxes. Citizens may measure county officials by the speed and frequency with which their own personal desires for special treatment are met. County officials daily confront wrathful constituents interested in the next favor of the official, not a resume of past services.

An extraordinary kinship does develop between county officials and their political clients that perpetuates a reasonably amicable interchange of pressures, compromises, favors, and services. Rigid legal restrictions on the discretion of county government make politically special relationships necessary to compensate for the lack of formal rule making and administrative authority. Divided allegiance and dual state-local roles of some county officials further encourage informal, unorthodox, and highly personalized administrative styles and practices. State interests are usually filtered through the purely local perspective of county functionaries, ever aware of the growing restlessness of citizens who want taxes kept low, while continuing the same kinds of personal concern for their particular problems. The decentralization of administration and finance in Texas counties makes informal relations and arrangements inevitable. Without them, it would be difficult for Texas counties to function at all. The primary aim of all these relationships is to preserve the status quo as inexpensively as possible. Such understandings permit county government to operate as well as can be expected within the intractable restrictions of the Texas Constitution and ingrained county traditions. County officials and their subordinates constantly modify formal, routinized duties to provide services for citizens that preserve a solid base for continued reelection.

The Sheriff as Political Microcosm

Since frontier days in Texas, the sheriff has been a major political and law enforcement figure, even more so fifty years ago than today. The sheriff provides an excellent illustration of the complex interplay of formal and informal powers in county government. A hybrid entity, required to act simultaneously as an officer of county government and of state government, the sheriff is the principal officer with a county-wide constituency and contact with all components of the political system—local, state, and national. Accountable to all the county voters, the sheriff has been an important, and in some instances predominant, political figure. An aspirant for the office may achieve election with minimal technical requirements by being sufficiently popular (name identification) and remain in office by satisfying constituents in ways peculiar to the sheriff's office.

As the principal law enforcement officer of county government, the sheriff faces the multiplicity of choices which any officer of the law must make daily. He must frequently decide whether to enforce a state law literally or to make an exception as a justifiable adaptation of the letter of legislative intent to anticipated demands of voters. The sheriff casts his political bread on the waters and hopes that it will return to his benefit at election time.

A basic assumption of any appraisal of the politics of the Texas sheriff is that the office is uniquely affected by the imperatives of electoral democracy. The sheriff is the principal "good ole boy" of the county, with an extensive knowledge of voters' needs, priorities, and peculiarities; he is the number one "Mr. Fixit" and universal *pater familias* of the county. The personal service aspects of the sheriff's tasks intrude upon impartial and professional law enforcement with significant impact on getting elected and staying in office—shaping the sheriff as a social and professional institution. The sheriff is a lodestone and lightning rod of politics in a rapidly urbanizing, industrializing Texas, beset by myriad demographic and public policy changes and challenges.

The sheriff is an excellent laboratory for evaluating the conflict between old conceptions of public policy and the transformations of urban life. The sheriff is feeling all the transforming catalysts exerting themselves on other governments in Texas, plus some forces distinctively directed at the sheriff.

Texas has been nurtured by a philosophy of very limited government. The philosophy gets in the way of practical policy at every level of Texas' political system. Conventional wisdom often sees this merely as a persistent conservatism deterring constructive change. The sheriff is a major magnet for pressure to change. He adapts grudgingly, but he adapts.

In state governments and their political subdivisions, the constraints of the state constitution affect politics and policy making. Among the major influences in the drafting of the Texas Constitution were: the Civil War and Reconstruction, the general decline in the popularity of state legislatures in the 1870s, the Grange movement, and certain attributes of Jacksonian democracy (the election of most officials, short terms of office, frequent rotation in office, and the like). These motivating factors mingled in various ways in the Texas Constitution: in complex restraints on the discretion of the governor (Civil War resentments); through rigid fetters on legislative options (resentment of post-Civil War legislative excesses); strictures on the fiscal flexibility of all governments (Granger retrenchment pressures); and the election of all major officials of government (Jacksonian democracy). Nowhere are the limits on policy making initiative more drastic than on county governments.

In Texas, public policy is affected by a pervasive parochialism and localistic outlook which prevents state policy from deviating from the entrenched priorities of local governments. In a state that has been urbanized for over forty years, an all-encompassing ruralism persists, smacking of a strange blend of southern populism and Jacksonian democracy. The sheriff's office is in many ways the most illustrative preserver and instrumentality of some of these characteristics. Vestiges of these ancient trappings remain visible in this institution which is adapting to some of the most rigorous pressures for change.

Any appraisal of the politics of the Texas sheriff would have to look beneath his daily civil, criminal, and custodial activities to raise some of the following queries: how do the personal service aspects of citizen demands impinge upon the temporal resources of the sheriff and upon general law enforcement operations? What kinds of demands for personal services come from constituents which have little to do with professional law enforcement? How are these things dealt with and with what effects on the whole skein of formal responsibilities for the sheriff? How do the elective sheriffs perceive their roles in the very human side of the office and their effects upon their functional ecology and their retention of an adequate political consensus? Even partial answers to these queries afford insights into the politics of the office as it has been and as it is becoming.

Certain presuppositions might underlie a pursuit of the politics of the Texas sheriff. Primary among these premises are the assumptions that (1) the office of Texas sheriff is more a custodial management, political office than a technical, professional law enforcement agency; (2) the constituents of the sheriff evaluate the office and its incumbent more on the basis of personal, political considerations than technical, law enforcement standards; and (3) of the constitutional officials of Texas county government, the sheriff best illustrates the grass roots, rurally oriented remnants of Jacksonian democracy.

The following summary leading to conclusions about the above premises is distilled from interviews with rural and urban sheriffs in Texas. The perceptions span the period from the late 1920s and early 1930s, a very important transitional period between the days when the sheriff still operated out of his saddle bags, to present-day urban sheriffs with fleets of helicopters, cars, speedboats, computers, airplanes, and college degrees.

Rural Sheriffs: Findings and Impressions

One gets the strong impression that of all county officials the sheriff is closest to his constituents. In rural areas, this intimacy has a two-pronged utility, in criminal law enforcement and in electoral politics. The detailed knowledge which some veteran sheriffs have of their citizens is phenomenal. This familiarity includes knowledge of the *modus operandi* of native criminals, which is useful locally and enhances assistance to fellow officers in other counties. Street sense about constituents permits the anticipation of people's needs. The sheriff is often the first person people come to for governmental assistance for any problem. The sheriff must listen sympathetically, give counsel, and take action. When he can resolve the problem himself, he will. He is expected to do so.

To contact most other county officials, the citizen must "come to town" to the courthouse. These meetings can be austerely formal and face the citizen with long waiting lines and the impersonal defensiveness of courthouse bureaucracies, all within the dreary, dingy mausoleum aura of many county courthouses. By contrast, the sheriff often greets people out in the county: on the street corner, in the favorite cafe watering places, in the fields, on the open highway, and locales conducive to relaxed associations and off-the-cuff confidences. When the sheriff himself is not at these places, his motorized deputies will be; most deputies are home county boys too. The politically savvy sheriff hires deputies who are sensitive to how their actions magnify the good will accruing to the boss. Stricter state certification requirements for deputies have not completely obviated this political perspective of sheriffing. Thus, the sheriff is departmentally much closer to his people. His saliency persists at a higher level than other county officials, simultaneously both an asset and a liability.

In the old days, a sheriff might put in an appearance at each of the little towns in his county every week, emphasizing the personal presence. A sheriff in what is now an urban county informed the author that he *still* drives around his county on weekends, stopping to chat with farmers in the field and table-hopping in county restaurants. It is interesting to note the extent to which rural people have not changed much in their response to this sort of treatment, though it is getting more difficult for even small county sheriffs to find time for this approach. A good relationship with opinion leaders and businessmen redounds favorably to sheriffs in the selection of criminal juries, possibly making it easier to get convictions in criminal cases. One former Texas sheriff felt that it was easier in the "old days" to get the cooperation of citizens in criminal investigations. The "don't want to get involved" syndrome seems to have penetraed the boondocks, a harbinger of creeping urbanism.

All rural sheriffs agreed that it was absolutely essential to know their citizens and to bend the political and professional dimensions of the office toward capitalizing on this knowledge. Estimates among small county sheriffs of the amount of time spent in dealing with personal citizen appeals for aid, advice, protection, and conversation ran from ten percent to two-thirds of a work day. One sheriff asserted that at least four hours every day were spent in head-to-head conversations with constituents without the remotest connection with law enforcement. The chief deputy of a West Texas county tells of a little old lady who calls him nearly every morning before he goes to work. She *may* have some problem, but generally, she is just lonely. Several sheriffs relate some variation of this story (including little old men). The time spent listening is not only a kindness, in some instances the person may be a respected elder of a prolific clan full of voters. The veteran sheriff of a small East Texas county referred to several nuclear families in his bailiwick; if the sheriff unduly antagonizes one of these peple, he may snowball five hundred votes against him.

A selective list of personal service demands made directly upon sheriffs would include such things as: (1) intercession for parents with teenage kids in trouble; this takes the form of a sort of youth counseling, plus keeping incidents from becoming public, a distinctive example of selective law enforcement; (2) demands to drive across the county to deliver a death notice; (3) requests to shadow a spouse and witness against the miscreant in divorce proceedings; (4) mediation in a multiplicity of family squabbles; (5) giving marital counseling and business advice; (6) rescuing cats from trees and muzzling barking dogs; (7) keeping the drinking problems of prominent citizens from public scrutiny; (8) preventing a dispute over a fence six inches over a property line from erupting into a shooting; and (9) providing funeral escorts. This list is only partial.

The author actually sat in the office of a small county sheriff and heard the sheriff's end of a fascinating conversation. The sheriff responded to the caller's entreaties in serious, even chivalrous tones. Apparently the lady caller was distressed because wolves had entered her hog pens and consumed a couple of prize porkers. She feared that the wolves were rabid, and the sheriff was admonished to do something, *pronto*. The sheriff responded as though he were talking to the local banker reporting a robbery in progress. The perturbed lady ws quietly reassured that the odds were high that her predator was a mother wolf with hungry pups, rather than mad. The sheriff gave detailed advice on setting traps for mother wolf, even suggesting that the traps be baited with wolf's urine, if possible.

Several minutes were taken in the exchange, with never a hint in the sheriff's voice that he was amused, bemused, or irritated at his time being taken up with such marginal criminal activities. The sheriff ranked the urgency of this situation with a similar request he had received during the same week to drive to the *far side* of the county and kill a stray "wild" cat for the lady of another farm family. The matriarch informed the sheriff that she was at home with nobody to help her but her "boy." When he asked the age of the "boy," the anxious mama replied that he was thirty-two. While the sheriff was pondering how to handle this dire criminal situation, the woman's "boy" took a shotgun and permanently calmed the felonious feline. This might be only rustically amusing, except that this county is contiguous with the most populous county in Texas and is beginning to "enjoy" a large spill-over of criminal activity from its big neighbor. The smaller county is a lake and resort area, where

Courtesy of *The Texas Lawman*

Sheriff Louis H. (Son) Hall, Sr., Stephens County, 1977-present

burglary cases have greatly proliferated. This small county sheriff has diminishing time for the kind of good ole boy, personalized touch demanded by the incidents just related. This evolution is becoming more noticeable in counties still considered to be rural.

The sheriff has to be more patient and discreet than any other county official, because he accumulates more inside information about people than any other public servant. Disclosed indiscriminately, this information might hurt people unnecessarily and undermine confidence in the sheriff. Each sheriff must judge this sort of thing carefully, because it can have political and law enforcement repercussions. This means that he must take a little time, let them talk, listen sympathetically, even if there is not a thing that can be done and no law to be enforced. Meticulous care must be taken to consider each citizen as an individual who cannot be treated like the others. Without such a personal touch, a man in a rural county may not remain sheriff very long. This personal touch probably has a salubrious effect on the basic respect for the law—at least, the law as reflected in the indigenous mores of each county.

A skillful sheriff may convince his county that it cannot do without him, and that if he were replaced, the "black hats" would take over. The continuing prevalence of this tactic is noteworthy, though it is noticeably dying with the attrition of long-term sheriffs. Many sheriffs made their reputation through initial toughness (in some instances, of the old West, shoot-'em-up variety) and remained in office through "taking care of my people" and convincing constituents that nobody else could do it. A retired sheriff told the author that if he had charged a fee, he would be a multi-millionaire through advice and personal services dispensed over thirty-four years in office. The sheriff epitomizes government for rural folk.

Urban Sheriffs - Perceptions

The day of the big county sheriff who personally "leads" his men in the field has passed. Urban counties are experiencing a transition from the boots and saddles sheriff who can always be approached personally to an office-bound administrator using the same management techniques as the metropolitan chief of police. The urban county sheriff is rapidly evolving from a seat-of-the-pants, good ole boy operation, to a full-scale professional law enforcement agency, with sophisticated organization and more prisoners in his jail than the general population of some Texas counties. Texas has some counties of immense geographic proportions and meager populations, all with the basic machinery of the sheriff's establishment.

A casualty of modernization and growth is the closeness between the sheriff and his constituents. Much of the big county's population has emigrated from the country, and for a while expects to contact the sheriff directly, resenting being referred to a deputy specializing in their problem. Ironically, television public service spots in some metropolitan areas tell citizens to call the sheriff's office when they need help. This does not usually get them the sheriff himself. The staff screens out and responds to many personal service appeals that are the direct, personal fare of rural sheriffs. The urban sheriff discovers that older sheriffs from smaller counties often think they should talk directly to him, as in the simpler days when the legendary Bill Decker (Dallas county) and Buster Kern (Harris County) sat with open doors and took time to "stroke" the sheriff from the sticks when he came in for business.

In the urban counties, people look upon the sheriff more as a law enforcement agency and less as a personal trouble-shooting mentor. The politics of the urban sheriff is increasingly swept up in sophisticated public relations and participation in ribbon cuttings, speech making

Courtesy of *The Texas Lawman*, Sheriffs Association of Texas, Austin, Texas

C.V. (Buster) Kern, former sheriff,
Harris County, Texas, 1951-1973

(hundreds), banquets, civic organizations, a running interchange with the press, and enthusiastic assistance to big charity fund raising. One of the most respected former sheriffs in Texas' largest county, noted for his abilities as a criminal investigator, stated that he had spent many hours in non-law enforcement activities, such as: deputizing the Borden Company's prize bull, Beauregard; judging human beauty contests; crowning queens of everything; even kissing Dorothy Lamour.

Most of the big county sheriff's time is now spent in administration and personnel management, and the key to being a good sheriff is maintaining a good staff of skilled professionals. There is a growing divergence between the politics of the urban sheriff and the rural sheriff. For the rural sheriff, *everything* is political, even crimes. The present incumbent in the state's largest county estimated that his constituents probably evaluated his performance fifty percent on professional law enforcement and fifty percent on politics. In the rural counties, the ratio is probably ten percent to ninety percent. Still, if the best peace officer in the world neglected the up-front public relations facet of the urban sheriff, he would be bounced out of office. From this standpoint, it appears to be more difficult to stay in office than to attain it originally.

In the very populous counties, there are thousands of "name voters" who endorse candidates persistently seen on the ballot for years, with little or no knowledge about professional demands on incumbents. Judicious delegation of law enforcement authority and citizen contact becomes a key to the successful urban sheriff. The urban sheriff decreasingly hears the individualized *"help me"* entreaties that are the substance of politics for the hinterland sheriff. Both urban and rural sheriffs may get citizens' calls that begin with: "Sheriff, I voted for you, but you don't know me," or: "Jack, I voted for you last election, but I don't know if I can support you again next time, unless...," or: "J.B., I was glad to vote for you last election, here's my problem."

Presumably this puts the sheriff in a responsive mood, talking to a real supporter, or subtly threatens him with withholding a vote, if the sheriff does not react properly. The sheriff *never* gets a call from someone who voted *against* him.

The Politics of Intergovernmental Relations

Every sheriff learns that partisan, political factors affect the flow of money to his department from the county budget. This fact of life enhances the importance of amicable relations with other institutions of government, especially the county commissioners, who determine the sheriff's operational funds. Texas' separation of finance and administration at the county level makes fiscal concerns a special reason for a sheriff to remain politically strong in a general sense. The sheriff will often be the most influential political figure in any county. He is the official with the most comprehensive county-wide constituency. As his county grows in population and industrial complexity, however, the sheriff discovers that it is harder to preserve political clout *and* fight crime. As his county grows, law enforcement efficiency becomes more important to maintaining political good health. In most Texas counties, the county commissioners court competes with the sheriff as the focal repository of political influence, though each commissioner represents only one precinct. The county judge (also with a county-wide constituency) may compete with the sheriff for political predominance, not always successfully. The primary pressure on commissioners in allocating county funds is to provide for roads and bridges. Fostering his own priorities is a constant struggle for the sheriff, with commissioners who are not law enforcement oriented. The separation of finance and administration complicates the politics between the sheriff and county commissioners. The

Courtesy of Harris County Sheriff's Department

Sheriff Jack Heard, Harris County, 1973-present.
Currently sheriff of the state's largest, most
metropolitan county.

sheriff's money is determined by county commissioners, but the commissioners have no jurisdiction over the sheriff's functional powers, which come from state law.

In the 1970s, pressure from federal courts and a burgeoning state regulatory bureaucracy to divert larger resources into jail improvement heightened political tension and greatly increased the frequency of contact between the sheriff and the county commissioners. Pressure on the sheriff to improve his jail or face federal judicial or state administrative shut down of the county's detention facilities enabled the sheriff to shift the onus of expensive jail modifications from himself to county commissioners. This is one aspect of the separation between finance and administration that can work positively in sheriff's politics. County taxpayers, who do not cheerfully face rising property taxes for more commodious quarters for felons, can be told by the sheriff that he is merely following state law and playing Horatio at the bridge where federal judges cross to dip into citizens' business and pocketbooks. Pressures from outside political systems on jail standards have magnified the intensity of the spotlight on the sheriff, thus giving him additional opportunities to make political and electoral hay. The sheriff often portrays himself as the major bulwark between the home folks and outlander Armageddons always ominously imminent. The responses of Texas sheriffs since 1972 to the impetus for jail improvement show sheriffs to be institutionally very adaptable to irresistible change. More on this subject will be said later in this essay.

The central role played by the sheriff in criminal law enforcement and in civil process sometimes leads other state agencies to forget that they also exercise authority in the same areas. The sheriff usually takes the lead, working from his central position in the local law enforcement system. In certain crimes, the sheriff, city police, constable, and Texas Rangers have concurrent jurisdiction. In the big cities, municipal police would probably take charge of an investigation within city limits. This procedure is not so likely in the rural areas.

Some very interesting political techniques of the sheriff occur in criminal investigations. The rural sheriff may consider the advantage of intervening personally in a criminal investigation. In cases with political advantage (good press), sheriffs may assume control, first making certain that the case can be easily solved. Professional jealousy and petty conflicts may erupt in concurrent inquiries, with a race to capture credit in the local press. The chase may be on between a chief of police and the sheriff, or between the sheriff and another sheriff. In easy cases without serious political ramifications, the agency of traditional responsibility handles the case without requesting or wanting outside aid. In hard cases or politically sensitive cases, the Department of Public Safety (Texas Rangers) may be called in, becoming an ideal scapegoat for local buck passing. All the sheriff has to do to shift the responsibility is to make it known that he has called in the state. The public expects more of the state officers, who are assumed to command superior expertise. The focus of attention can thus be shifted from the sheriff in potentially onerous cases.

A common device for the sheriff in delicate cases is the "put off." The sheriff informs complaining constituents that their problem has been submitted to the grand jury for consideration. This is especially useful with complaints by one constituent against another (anathema for an elected lawman). Since the deliberations of the grand jury are secret, the complainant rarely learns if the information was actually submitted. This technique is also practical when the sheriff does not want to tell a constituent that his complaint is frivolous.

Sheriffs are quick to invoke their position as chief law enforcement officer when it is to their advantage. The pluses and minuses must be weighed. Sheriffs are not required to have any professional training prior to election. Some persons become sheriff with little prior experience in law enforcement, often inducing political caution in criminal cases. A large percentage of current sheriffs *has* previous enforcement experience. A sheriff must follow a sensitive protocol in criminal cases; his authority extends to any place in the county, including incorporated cities. Discretion demands that he stay out of the way of municipal police departments capable of handling their own criminal cases as a matter of the general good will which the hyper-political sheriff must preserve.

Occasionally, miffed feelings arise between two sheriffs, leading to a sort of one-upmanship in their usually cooperative relations. Examples of retaliatory actions are: refusal to execute another sheriff's processes in the county, refusal to intercede on behalf of another sheriff's constituents, or keeping a prisoner after he has already been warranted to another sheriff's jurisdiction or to the Texas Department of Corrections. Generally, in criminal matters, if a sheriff is a good coordinator, he can get things done by mobilizing all the state and local authorities for results that satisfy the law and the voters.

General Conclusions on the Politics of the Sheriff

The three main suppositions underlying this view of the politics of the Texas sheriff seem to be confirmed. The Texas sheriff *is* primarily a custodial management and political office, rather than a technically neutral, professional law enforcement entity, especially in the rural counties. In this, the rural sheriff is both a symptom and an instrumentality. The balance moves more heavily toward a crime fighting emphasis as the population of the county grows. Shrinking unincorporated territory in some counties affects the scope of the sheriff's activities, without really reducing his formal, legal powers.

There appears little doubt that constituents evaluate sheriffs by criteria that are personal and political in nature, rather than through objective, technical law enforcement standards. This approach is more manifest in the smaller counties. Vestigial Jacksonian democracy is revealed in the highly personalized, particularized character of relations between citizen and sheriff; in the persistent pressure to continue election of sheriffs as the "people's" lawman; in the exemption of the sheriff from state professional qualifications for peace officer certification, which are strictly required of all deputies; in the process of choosing deputies, which continues to reflect elements of the spoils system in spite of state certification standards; and the expressed belief in the ultimate efficacy of the people's judgment that is the root of pressure to preserve the sheriff as an institution. There is an unusual symbiosis between the sheriffs and their people, and future modifications of county governments in Texas must be rooted in a rational adjustment to this phenomenon of political biology.

The realities of the sheriff's image lie somewhere between a grotesque literary caricature, a worse threat to lawfulness than any of his quarry, and the white-hatted paragon of 1930s films.

The Human Dimension of the Office: From Two-Fisted, Two-Gun Days to Modern Technological Professional

There is a fascinating relationship in our political system betwen the incumbent who holds a public office and the institutional developments of the office itself. No office demonstrates this complex interplay of causes and effects more than the Texas sheriff. The State of Texas is both southern and western in its political development, and the sheriff reflects this mottled amalgam very directly. The Anglo-American shrievalty has always been an important indicator of trends as successive regimes attempt to govern. The American federal system, with its remarkable division of powers and responsibilities among the constituent parts of government, has been a distinctive crucible within which the sheriff has responded to the forces of change and growth that were exerting themselves upon the nation and the state.

The shrievalty has from the first been both an object and an instrument in the evolution of forms, processes, and politics that has given us our present system of government and law enforcement. The sheriff functions at a strategic point in the governmental system, where he is the first to feel some of the winds of change emanating from the state capital and from elsewhere in the federal system. From this strategic vantage point, the sheriff acts as a determined resistor to those changes which his people do not want to accept. His dual role, as both an agent of local government and state government, enables him to use his unusual brand of discretion in law enforcement to modify and adapt changes intruding from the upper reaches of the system. The sheriff provides the citizens of his county a cushion of time to decide how much of their old ways can be preserved within a facade of compliance with inevitable and unavoidable adjustments. As creatures of the state, with no independent powers to legislate, county governments are particularly vulnerable to changes imposed from the outside, at least in a constitutional sense. The counties are not without political abilities to restrain the tendencies of the state legislature to enforce change too rapidly. The sheriff has often been a useful means of such protection.

In the less urban or outright rural counties, the sheriff's closeness to his constituents and his intimate knowledge of their folkways and political reflexes have heightened the sheriff's influence in the velocity of change. In studying the incidence of various kinds of reform in Texas, one is frequently struck by the degree of influence exerted against change by the combined political organizations of sheriffs, county judges, justices of the peace, county commissioners, and other elected officials of county government. Their impact is often out of proportion to the small numbers of people actually represented by their professional state organizations. The cumulative total of their respective elective constituencies represents a figure that state legislators have always respected. If one tries to understand why urbane, sophisticated, college-educated urban legislators respond consistently to the pressures coming from local officials, the basic answer lies in the solon's imagination. The legislator can easily visualize the supporters of these county officials mobilizing against him in the next election.

One of the most recent and illustrative policy areas where this interesting role of the sheriffs stands out is in the area of jail standards. In the 1970s, Texas counties were subjected to a host of suits in federal district courts, in which plaintiffs attacked county jail management standards of nearly two-hundred years. Under the Fourteenth Amendment of the United States Constitution, the physical condition of county jails and the accompanying management techniques were attacked as violative of the civil rights of jail inmates. Federal district court judges ordered sheriffs to up-grade their jails or face shut-downs by judicial fiat. Suddenly, sheriffs and county commissioners were devoting a vast amount of their resources, their time, and their political currency to an area of county operations which had always been a principal responsibility of the sheriff and treated as an administrative step-child, even by the sheriff.

Under the threat of federal court injunctions, county commissioners and the sheriffs were faced with the horror of presenting taxpaying voters with immense, multi-million dollar bond elections to underwrite new jails and sweeping improvements of old facilities, some of which had been built in the Nineteenth Century. Here was a force for change that was not going to go away and which was not subject to the modifying effects of law enforcement discretion.

Consequently, new state laws were passed which created an entire new state administrative system for promulgating statewide standards for jail construction and administration...the State Commission on Jail Standards. The legislation creating the new system was largely influenced by the sheriffs, and the new Commission would be required by statute to have two sheriffs as members, one from a rural county and one from an urban county. From the start of the new system, the sheriffs worked closely with the new Commission and its field inspectors, modifying rigorous new standards wherever possible, to permit an easier transition for the counties from the old era of benign neglect to the new era of scrutiny by the double-eyed supervision of federal courts and the new state regulatory machinery. This new point of contention found the sheriffs caught in a squeeze-play. On one side were the federal courts, with their constant threat of inmate suits, and the new state jail commission, with powers to promulgate and enforce new state standards. On the other hand were the county commissioners, acting as both a channel for change and source of pressures to resist or hold to a minimum the monumental increases in local property taxes that the new changes would make necessary.

Jail standards politics of the past decade illustrates graphically the role of the sheriff simultaneously cushioning his county from outside forces while permitting the inevitable changes to be made as painlessly as possible. One could not conjure up a better illustration of the vital adaptability of the office of sheriff which has helped it to survive institutionally for nearly a thousand years. Exercising centuries of conditioned reflexes, sheriffs were initially against the new wave of jail standards changes, but they wound up as major participants in determining the form and velocity of changes that could not be avoided. Through it all, the institutional sheriff survives.

The jail standards issue is merely the most noticeable of a myriad of alterations that have spread throughout our criminal justice system in the past two decades. Many of the incumbents in the office when these changes began have been replaced. Some grudgingly gave in when they could no longer prevent the new developments, making way for younger sheriffs who will exercise the augmented but transformed roles of the sheriff and who will have to take the office through the rest of this century into the next.

Dramatis Personae

Almost every Texas county has several dramatic individuals who have been sheriff. These individuals reflect both the good and the pathological about the office in Texas history. In their careers and personalities, one can see the outlines of the stereotypical western sheriff, blown bigger than life by the imaginations of Hollywood. In these sheriffs one can note the inaccuracies and outright misrepresentations that compose much of the imagery of Nineteenth Century dime novels and more recent portrayals of the sheriff on film. The "High Noon Syndrome" fosters a mostly incorrect impression of early western communities and of the efforts to establish what was accepted as law and order in virtually all American communities in the Nineteenth Century. For the most part, the lack of law or order and the accompanying roles of the western peace officer in these evolving conditions have been severely exaggerated. Still, most myths have some degree of foundation in fact.

The emergence of the western peace officer is a distinctive part of the development of modern police systems in the entire United States. The peculiar combination of geography and economics that characterized the West certainly made for some uniquely indigenous practices and emphases in western law enforcement. In Texas, the county governmental system of the Old South was particularly important as a basis for local government and law enforcement. The sheriff was transplanted intact with the earliest waves of caucasian immigrants from the southland. The role types and operational tasks of the sheriff were part and parcel of local history, as the office evolved from a seat-of-the-pants, work out of the saddle bags office to a big time operation on a par with the big city police department and unique connections with every level of the American law enforcement system.

There are as many types of individuals filling the office of Texas sheriff as there are counties in the state. Many of these individuals differ from the stereotyped image of the western (Texas) sheriff. Some of them are fat, balding, and well *under* six feet in height. Some are lean and trim as a whippet. Some affect the ten gallon hat and cowboy boots, in combination with business suit, or with white shirt and blue jeans. Some present the owlish appearance of the "typical" television college professor or accountant, whom one would hardly distinguish from the ordinary run of businessman seen daily on the streets of any Texas city. In some jurisdictions where the sheriff's deputies wear uniforms, the sheriff himself will usually wear a regular business suit (perhaps with the Stetson and cowboy boots). Increasingly, some police jurisdictions, including sheriff's departments, are trying to move away from the western flair by prohibiting the wearing of cowboy boots. In age, the sheriffs run from very young men to grandfathers in their seventies.

Personalities of sheriffs are as varied as the geographic and economic differences of their counties. Some sheriffs fall into the reticent, Gary Cooper category as men of very few words; others are garrulous, extroverted men who fit easily into any group and who relish and frequently use the spotlight of public attention.

In addition to great variety in physical attributes and personal styles, personal sketches of sheriffs disclose family dynasties, with grandfather, father, and son combinations following each other in the office; Republican sheriffs (shades of the formerly solid South); sheriffs with incredibly long tenure; sheriffs killed in the line of duty; black sheriffs; members of the same family simultaneously serving as sheriff in different counties; and some Texas sheriffs have been (are) women. In some of the smaller counties it is not unheard of for the widow of a sheriff who dies in office to succeed her husband.

When one asks incumbent sheriffs and other law enforcement agents about "the great" sheriffs, certain names are mentioned without hesitation. Bill Decker of Dallas County and Buster Kern of Harris County both lived long enough to see themselves pictured as living legends. Each man represents the small body of urban sheriffs whose careers occurred at an historical point where the urban sheriff shook off the vestiges of the frontier and entered the era of law enforcement created by modern technology. Tarrant County Sheriff Lon Evans, an ex-Green Bay Packers star, is probably the last living big-county sheriff in this category. Internationally renowned, and active in national sheriffs' organizations, Sheriff Evans now runs his modern law enforcement organization from a wheel chair after having had a leg amputated. He is the center of attention and treated with great respect by his colleagues at the annual meeting of the Sheriffs Association of Texas.

Bill Decker was the last of the big county sheriffs to "lead his men in the field," personally participating in criminal investigations and arrests. The Dallas County sheriff now functions as an office-bound administrator, presiding over a huge organization of deputies, forensic specialists, criminal investigators, patrolmen, a small army of civil deputies, and a large civilian staff. The same could be said several times over for Sheriff Jack Heard of Harris County (Houston), who entered the office with an extensive and varied career in law enforcement for the State of Texas and the City of Houston. Sheriff Heard's predecessor, the legendary Buster Kern, developed a nation-wide reputation as a criminal investigator, with a sixth sense about criminal behavior. Kern reflected a simultaneous appreciation for the impact of the western image and the utility of modern forensic science and technology. Vestiges of the relationships which rural sheriffs still maintain were an important part of the early careers of Decker and Kern, producing a very personal character in their administration. Their successors have seen the big county office go completely over the line into a modern, metropolitan police force, while experiencing the same increases in custodial duties as their rural counterparts, brought on by jail standards issues of the 1970s. In the huge urban counties, the spreading incorporation of hitherto unincorporated land by the expanding metropolitan cities and their mushrooming bedroom cities has begun to have important effects on the territorial imperatives of the urban sheriff, even though his legal jurisdiction has not shrunk.

Equally interesting examples of the impact of industrialization and urbanization on previously rural counties can be found across the state. Some of these sheriffs are beginning to experience most of the transitional influences that were magnified proportionately in the urban sheriffs.

Two of these small county sheriffs are fascinating prototypes of the transitional Texas sheriff in the Twentieth Century, beginning their law enforcement careers at a time in which the sheriff had relatively little of the equipment of modern communications, transportation, detection, and records-keeping which almost every sheriff now has at his disposal. The late Jess Sweeten was sheriff of Henderson County (Athens) from 1933 to 1955, and the late T. J. (Big Jim) Flournoy was sheriff for thirty-four years in Fayette County (LaGrange, 1947-1980).

Each of these men might physically have been created in Hollywood. Sweeten was six feet four inches tall, and Flournoy is six feet six inches tall, both exceeding two hundred pounds in their seventies. Each man began his career in the tough and turbulent 1920s, when sheriffs still operated partially out of their saddle bags. Flournoy served for thirteen years as a deputy in his county before being elected sheriff. After his initial election in 1946, he rarely had an opponent for reelection. Flournoy served as a Texas Ranger long enough to be inaugurated into the Texas Ranger Hall of Fame. Sweeten began his career as a constable in the early East Texas oil fields, a very tough apprenticeship.

The career of both men was sculpted in their immense hands, with knuckles gnarled by innumerable contacts with the chins of men who resisted arrest. On countless weekends as young officers, they would fight all weekend subduing oil field workers who did not want to sleep it off in the county cooler. Several unrepentant and unwise felons were forced by these two sheriffs to sleep forever in the county cemetery, and a number of miscreants bled for their sins from wounds inflicted by the two deadly marksmen. Sweeten's living room wall is festooned with awards and photographs resulting from his exhibitions of marksmanship, many of them coming after he was already retired. Flournoy was said to begin each deer hunting season by centering his rifle sight by knocking the center out of several dozen bottle caps. The center of several lawbreakers was much larger.

Each man's speaking voice rumbled from somewhere in the depths of a ponderous midsection which had supported heavy sidearms for many years. Sheriff Flournoy even had to stop wearing one of his favorite guns when its weight caused rheumatism. The grandfatherly twinkle that flashed from their eyes when recounting an amusing incident from their career belied the formidable fiber underneath which permitted each man to face down a long chain of thugs covering a combined career of more than one hundred years. This intrinsic toughness had nothing to do with the hyperbole of dime novels; it was real and undeniably displayed in situations faced by small county sheriffs in East Texas.

Sheriff Sweeten's little great-granddaughter played lovingly at his feet as he recounted an incident to the author in which a man holed up in an old abandoned house with a rifle and began to shoot at passing motorists and pedestrians. Not wanting to endanger his deputies, Sweeten himself worked his way up to the front porch of the old shack. By listening to the squeaking of the floor boards, he could anticipate the movements of the sniper. When he had moved directly in front of the door, Sweeten kicked it in. In Sweeten's words, "He began to swing his rifle up to direct it at me." A pregnant pause in Sweeten's account, then he said with a sinister smile, "He was a bit too slow." In this fashion, both Sweeten and Flournoy developed a reputation for fearless protection of the public peace in their counties very early in their careers. Little wonder that Flournoy's county had the lowest crime rate of any county in the state in the year he retired. Each man developed a prodigious reputation, based on real and figurative notches in their guns. Once established, the control of the county became a complex matter of fostering the reputation and occasionally reminding a few hardheads that the reputation was not fictitious.

Sweeten and Flournoy represent a "shoot-em'up" strain in the sheriff which was often a factor in what the old-time sheriff considered "enforcing the law," even though the fast gun facet of the western peace officer was mostly Hollywood hype. The ability and willingness of these two small county sheriffs to use a gun, or a fist, or a flashlight on those who intruded upon their county's assumptions of propriety were not exaggerated.

There is an "atmosphere" that surrounds each of these old officers, an aura of an eerie nature, which is only partly impressed upon a stranger by their reputation. The emanation of power and, if necessary, meanness, still impressed strangers with these two men when they were nearly eighty years old. The aura is one of a potential ruthlessness and utter fearlessness, augmented by the physicl size of each man. A citizen of LaGrange once recommended to an outsider that he look in Sheriff Flournoy's eyes. When contemplating anything threatening to his people, those eyes glowered with a hellish blackness and coldness that chilled one's blood, even when he was retired and approaching his eightieth birthday. The thought of federal judges and their favoring suits against sheriffs could precipitate this baleful countenance. Both men expressed regret at not being able to kill Bonnie and Clyde, a recurrent preoccupation with East Texas lawmen from the 1930s. Sweeten said that Bonnie and Clyde were the only felons he had hoped to get a chance to shoot. Fifty years later, Sweeten asked for divine forgiveness for this unChristian thought, but the listener did not doubt that he would have done it. Sweeten told of the notorious pair's murder of two young Texas highway patrolmen with a venomous clarity as though the deed had happened yesterday, not fifty years ago.

Sweeten told of having to go to Austin to return a member of the Bonnie and Clyde gang to Athens for trial. Accompanied by a deputy, Sweeten proposed to drive the swaggering hood back to Henderson County. The bank robber bragged that Bonnie and Clyde would rescue him before they got to Henderson County. Sweeten said,

"Sonny boy, I hope they try, because I've got a plan. I'm going to sit you in the front seat beside my deputy. I'm going to ride in the back with my shotgun and other weapons. When they make their move to rescue you, I'm first going to *blow your head off*. Then, I'll turn to old Bonnie and Clyde, and I'll get them, because I'm better than they are." The hood, upon looking into those eyes, melted into the front seat and prayed against the rescue attempt. His prayers were answered, and Sweeten got his man back to the county for trial.

Both Flournoy and Sweeten remembered numerous incidents of their careers in which the lack of modern technological equipment hampered criminal investigations. Sweeten told of how he missed capturing the nefarious Bonnie and Clyde by ten minutes in his county because he had no radio in his patrol car to inform officers in adjoining counties that the murderous duo was headed their way. These two rural county sheriffs, whose counties were feeling the brunt of urbanization, showed a strong appreciation for modern investigative techniques and equipment, even though they had both relied during much of their careers upon an instinctive and practical code built upon experience and an extensive knowledge of people. Flournoy's motto with respect to lawbreakers was "Get the SOB, one way or another." He usually did. Both men were proud that there was never an unsolved murder or major felony in their counties during their tenure.

Sweeten and Flournoy epitomized the human discretion that every peace officer must utilize in shaping the enforcement of the letter of the law to fit the felt needs of their constituents and their communities. The sheriff applies this complex process of discretion in a completely unique fashion. Each man developed a deep-seated protectiveness for his county and its people, against both the criminal elements and any part of the political system that might adversely intrude upon the way of life of their county. The service aspect of the office of sheriff, previously discussed, is very noticeable in the careers of these two traditional Texas sheriffs. For example, at the outbreak of World War Two, Jess Sweeten talked a merchant out of pressing burglary changes against two young men, both of whom had been accepted by the Army. The sheriff knew that a criminal charge would prevent the Army from inducting the two boys, branding them irrevocably. Both young men survived the war and became exemplary citizens in the county. This was the same officer who calmly shot several men to death in the line of duty.

Sheriff Flournoy is famous nationwide for his defense of his county and its particular traditions when the state forced the closing down of the famous Chicken Ranch. The Chicken Ranch, a noted house of prostitution since 1844, was closed down as a result of pressure from the state governor and a big city television campaign in 1973. Publicity focused upon the incident by Houston television personalities led to lawsuits against the sheriff and the county. The county rallied behind Sheriff Jim, taking up money for his defense fund and otherwise manifesting appreciation for his fifty years of protectiveness. One could not ask for a better example of a sheriff in his capacity as protector of the county and its traditions against pressures from the outside, regardless of the specific problems of law enforcement that the sheriff might face. The Chicken Ranch incident encapsulates the extensive political and personal power which some sheriffs have been able to exert, convincing their constituents that without them, the black hats move in. This phenomenon is undoubtedly a factor in the very long tenure in office of Sheriff Flournoy and others. Sheriff Flournoy's younger brother, Mike, developed a similar situation in Wharton County twenty years before his death.

In many interviews before their retirement, Sheriff Sweeten (who died in 1980) and Sheriff Flournoy (who died in 1982) complained of the difficulties of "enforcing the law" after the advent of civil rights suits on behalf of prisoner rights. Both men had compiled very successful records in criminal investigations and management of crime rates in their counties before the sheriff had to be concerned with civil suits against him and his methods. When both men found it no longer possible to adapt, they got out. Perhaps their counterpart in West Texas is Big Ed Darnell of Midland County, who has been retired for some years now.

The successors to these men will be different. They may or may not be more successful. The criteria for success as a sheriff will probably undergo a serious transformation. In the rural areas, it will not come as soon, but the changes are reaching quickly throughout the state. In 1978, at their annual state meeting, the Sheriffs Association of Texas recommended that the elected sheriff be required to have the same qualifications as certified peace officers as their deputies must now have. Eventually, the legislature will enact such legislation.

Concluding Observations

What is the prospective future of the county sheriff in Texas? Can the office adapt to the changing complexion of intergovernmental relations and the heightening competition for scarce resources? What is the viable role of the sheriff in the long-range future of law enforcement and politics n Texas? Is the Texas sheriff a model of modern law enforcement or a political anachronism? It is not possible to give definitive answers to any of these questions, but it is not likely that the office is going to disappear any time soon. The Anglo-American sheriff has been too hardy and resilient to write off as an anachronism with absolutely no place in the scheme of Texas history.

Texas has twenty-five standard metropolitan statistical areas, more than any other state in the United States. Included in these metropolitan areas are fifty-three of Texas' counties, or about twenty percent of the 254 counties. The map of Texas is still covered with hundreds of smaller incorporated areas and unincorporated cities, with wide expanses of territory lying outside any municipal limits. Many of these smaller municipalities rely upon the sheriff's organization for law enforcement, patrol, and custodial services...in some instances, on the basis of a yearly, written contract. For these areas, the sheriff will continue to be an important agency, both professionally and politically.

Where urbanization has been the greatest, the emphasis upon crime fighting, general law enforcement, and custodial responsibilities for the sheriff has increased enormously. The number of areas in the state where the boundaries of the huge, megalopolis and the county are almost coterminous is small, even though a large proportion of the state's population is beginning to live in these areas. Here, the sheriff is showing remarkable ability to adapt to new professional demands. The impetus toward evaluating the sheriff more on professional law enforcement criteria and less on the personalized, political criteria of the rural counties is growing. The sheriff in the great metropolitan counties is becoming more like a large city chief of police, except for his continued selection by the voters. The responsibility for jail management is growing across the state, and not many municipal leaders are volunteering to take over this function for the system. The greatest changes are taking place directly in the office of the sheriff, as he becomes less a politial field general and more an office-bound administrator.

The historical adaptability of the sheriff is manifesting itself anew in the current upheavals of the state's transition into another century. The sheriff will continue to be an important official as long as Texas retains its huge number of counties, each with its own separate and complete machinery of county government. If Texas ever undertakes a consolidation of its multiplicity of counties into fewer, but larger county units, the number of sheriffs will certainly decline, but it is doubtful that the office will be eliminated. The professionalization that has been underway in municipal law enforcement during the past decade is making itself felt in a material way in the Texas sheriff. Once again, the wily old chameleon is changing his attire to the latest style. The belly may hang over the new beltline for a while, but a glance back over the last thousand years would suggest—not for long.

Suggested Additional Readings

British Background

1. Bryce Dale Lyon, *A Constitutional and Legal History of Medieval England* (New York: Harper & Bros., 1960).

2. John A. R. Marriott, *English Political Institutions* (London: Oxford Press, fourth edition, 1910).

3. William Alfred Morris, *The Medieval English Sheriff to 1300* (New York: Manchester University Press, Barnes & Noble, Inc., 1927).

4. William Stubbs, *The Constitutional History of England in its Origin and Development* (London: Oxford Press, 1891).

5. Geoffrey Templeman, *The Sheriffs of Warwickshire in the Thirteenth Century* (London: Oxford Press, 1948).

General Works on the American Sheriff and the Sheriff of Other States

1. Dana B. Brammer and James E. Hurley, *A Study of the Office of Sheriff in the United States: Southern Region 1967* (University, Mississippi: The University of Mississippi, 1968).

2. T. C. Esselstyn, "The Social Role of a County Sheriff, *Journal of Criminal Law, Criminology, and Police Science* 44 (July-August, 1953), 177-184.

3. Roger B. Handberg and Charles M. Unkovic, "Southern County Sheriffs: A Changing Political Institution," *Free Inquiry in Creative Sociology* 8 (May, 1980), 44-48.

4. Roger B. Handberg and Charles M. Unkovic, "Southern County Sheriffs: Multifaceted Law Enforcement Agents," *Journal of Police Science and Administration* 6 (September, 1978), 311-317.

5. Rogert B. Handberg and W. T. Austin, "County Sheriffs View Law Enforcement," *Police Chief* (October, 1977), 28-29.

6. John K. Hudzik and Jack R. Greene, "Organizational Identity and Goal Consensus in a Sheriff's Department: An Exploratory Inquiry," *Journal of Police Science and Administration* 5 (1977), 79-88.

7. Cyrus H. Karraker, *The Seventeenth Century Sheriff, A Comparative Study of the Sheriff in England and the Chesapeake Colonies, 1607-1689* (Chapel Hill: The University of North Carolina Press, 1930).

8. Thomas Penfield, *Western Sheriffs and Marshalls* (New York: Grossett and Dunlap, 1855).

9. Frank R. Prassel, *The Western Peace Officer: A Legacy of Law and Order* (Norman, Oklahoma: The University of Oklahoma Press, 1972).

10. "Our Frontier-Style Sheriffs Are Vanishing," *U.S. News and World Report*, (March 5, 1979), 58-59.

11. *The National Sheriff*, published bi-monthly by the National Sheriffs Association, 1250 Connecticut Avenue, Washington, D.C.

12. Truman Walrod, *The Role of Sheriff: Past-Present-Future*

(Washington, D.C., The National Sheriffs Association, 1968).

The Texas Sheriff

1. Wilbourn E. Benton, *Texas: Its Government and Politics*, 3rd ed., (Englewood Cliffs, N.J.: Prentice-Hall, Inc., 1972), pp. 27-29.

2. Edwin S. Davis, "Shedding Light on the Dark Continent: County Officials in Texas," *Public Service* (May, 1976).

3. James G. Dickson, Jr., "State Role in Jail Standards Administration Becoming Greater, More Specific," *The Texas Lawman* (May, 1976, 45-61.

4. James G. Dickson, Jr., "Judicial Impatience and Administrative Delay: The Latest Round in the Dallas County Jail Standards Litigation," *The Texas Lawman* (July, 1977), 28-38.

5. James G. Dickson, Jr., "Sheriffs, Jails, and Federal Courts: A Quandary of Administration," *Public Affairs Comment* (August, 1977).

6. James G. Dickson, Jr., "Communication Without Understanding: The Informal Interplay of Politics in Texas County Government," in Ernest Crain, Charles Deaton, and William Maxwell, *The Challenge of Texas Politics* (St. Paul: The West Publishing Company, 1980), pp. 347-355.

7. James G. Dickson, Jr., "Profile of Texas Sheriffs: A Changing Composite, *The Texas Lawman* (June, 1981), 12-15.

8. Allan S. Lindquist, *Jess Sweeten, Texas Lawman* (San Antonio: The Naylor Company, 1961).

9. Wallace C. Murphy, *County Government and Administration in Texas* (Austin: Bureau of Research in the Social Sciences, The University of Texas, 1933).

10. Robert E. Norwood, *Texas County Government: Let the People Choose* (Austin: The Texas Research League, 1970).

11. *The Texas Lawman,* published monthly by the Sheriffs Association of Texas, Twin Towers Office Building, Austin, Texas.

R0150190130 TXR   T
                  363.
                  282
                  D554

DICKSON, JAMES G
     POLITICS OF THE
TEXAS SHERIFF FROM
FRONTIER TO BUREAUCRACY